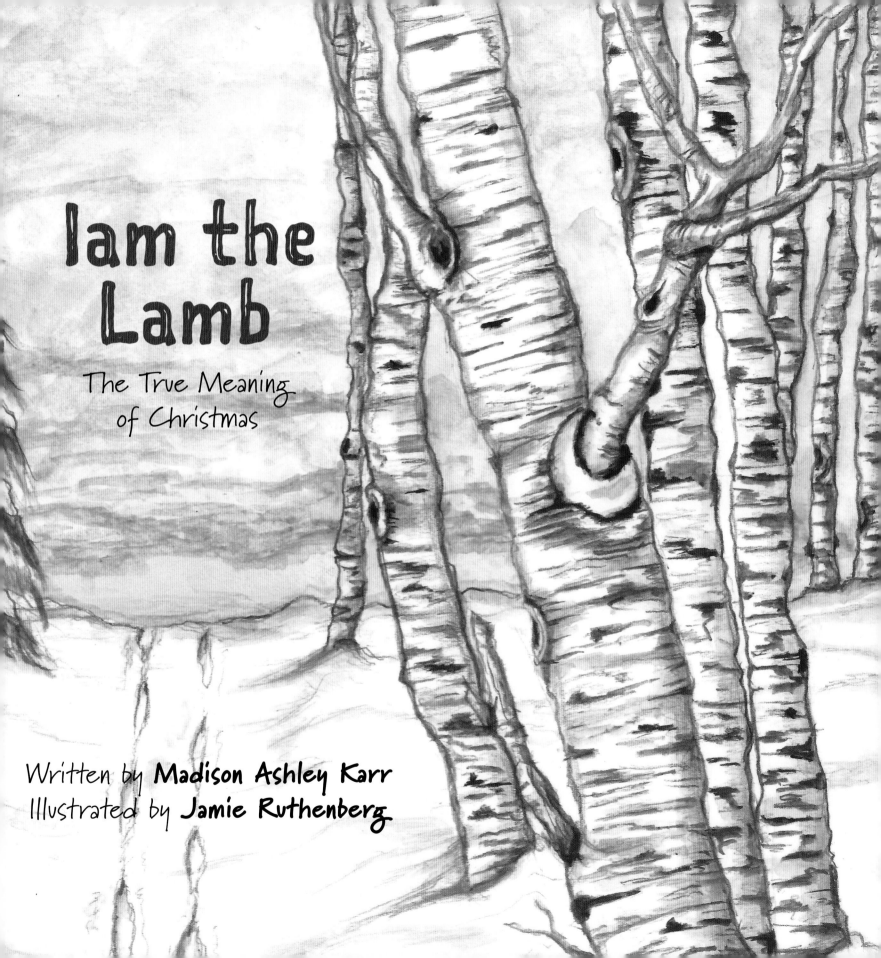

Iam the Lamb

The True Meaning of Christmas

Written by **Madison Ashley Karr**

Illustrated by **Jamie Ruthenberg**

ISBN: 978-1-7360754-0-1

Dedicated to my dear brothers, Joshua and Caleb Karr, who inspire me with their child-like faith every day. They have always had a tremendous love for Christmas.

And to my sister, Kallista Karr, who has the gentle spirit of a lamb. She is the most sheep-loving person I know.

When you think of Christmas what pops in your head?
Is it presents and cookies and canes white and red?

Or wreaths and stockings, or perhaps a little elf,
who quietly watches you as he sits on a shelf?

Do you think of Saint Nicholas, lights and a tree?
But could there be more to Christmas for you and for me?

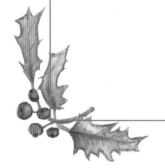

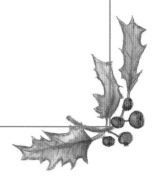
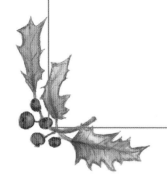

All of these traditions are such a joy to keep.
Each of these symbols have roots that run deep.

But I'm here to tell you there is so much more,
a center of focus that is more than folklore.

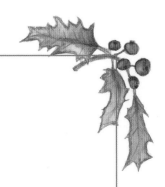
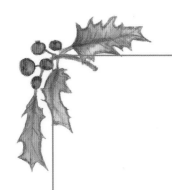

Before I tell you this story so sweet,
allow me to introduce myself, I am a sheep.

My name is Iam and I am the lamb so pure,
gentle and innocent, of this you can be sure.

I came here to spend this season with you,
and help you understand the meaning that's true.

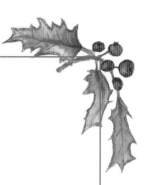
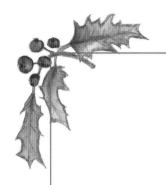

Yes! A symbol of Truth! That is the reason
I will be with you this Christmas season!

I'm here to show you the greatest gift of love
came from our Father in Heaven above.

Christmas is more than you see in the store.
It's about a baby named Jesus whom many adore.

Now let me tell you this amazing story,
how a baby was born to bring God's glory.

An angel came to tell a young girl named Mary
some incredible news that sounded quite scary.

But the angel told Mary, "Fear not favored one,
for you will give birth to God's Holy Son."

Jesus will be the baby boy's name.
On the throne of David, He will forever reign.

Mary responded, pondering all of this in her head,
"May it be unto me just as you have said."

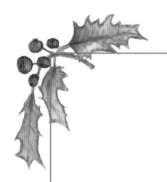

Then upon a donkey young Mary did ride.
Her husband named Joseph walked by her side.

To the town of Bethlehem, they had to travel.
There were many challenges they had to battle.

When they arrived, there was no room for them to stay.
So the baby was born in a stable filled with hay.

They placed Him in a manger amongst donkeys and sheep.
There was no other place for baby Jesus to sleep.

Angels rejoiced and shepherds came from afar,
along with three wise men who followed a star,
to see God's gift of love on the first Christmas night.
They knew Jesus was born to turn darkness to light.

Now every night before you go to bed,
think of all the places where light needs to be spread.

Because His light shines through you to everyone who sees,
throughout the world you can shine His love, joy, and peace.

By bringing joy to those who are broken and sad,
and love to children who need a mom or a dad.

By giving food and shelter to the needy and poor,
and a helping hand to the friend next door.

Now, throughout this season, go out and be bold.
Share this Christmas story to many untold.

For perfect is Jesus and I have come to say,
He is the true meaning for the Christmas holiday!

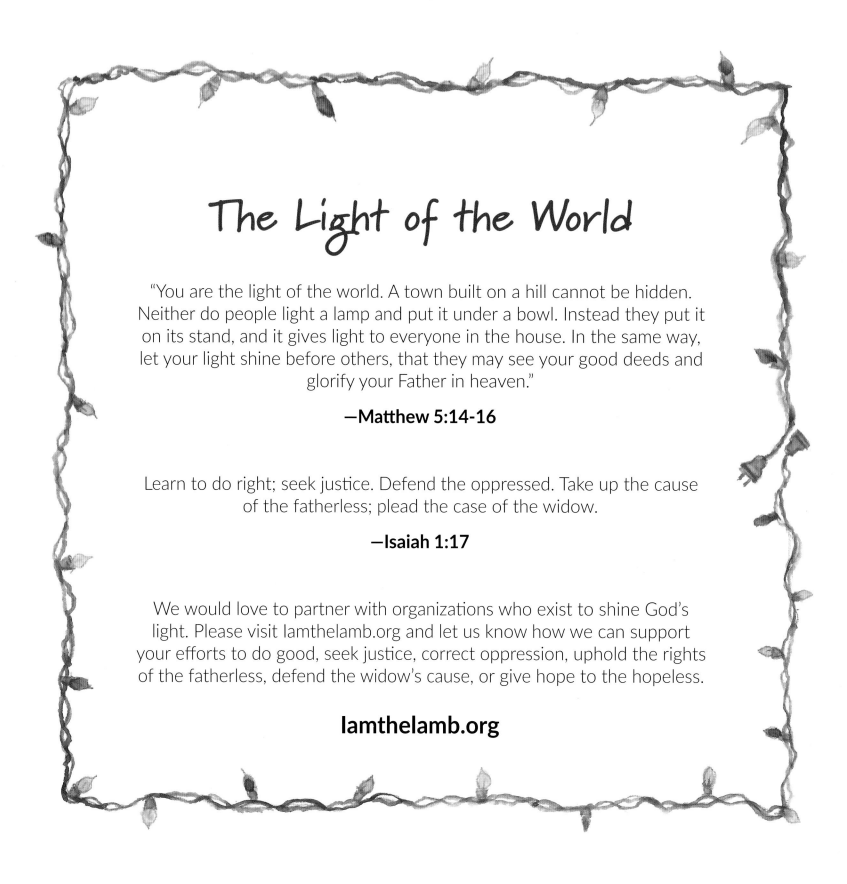

The Light of the World

"You are the light of the world. A town built on a hill cannot be hidden. Neither do people light a lamp and put it under a bowl. Instead they put it on its stand, and it gives light to everyone in the house. In the same way, let your light shine before others, that they may see your good deeds and glorify your Father in heaven."

—Matthew 5:14-16

Learn to do right; seek justice. Defend the oppressed. Take up the cause of the fatherless; plead the case of the widow.

—Isaiah 1:17

We would love to partner with organizations who exist to shine God's light. Please visit Iamthelamb.org and let us know how we can support your efforts to do good, seek justice, correct oppression, uphold the rights of the fatherless, defend the widow's cause, or give hope to the hopeless.

Iamthelamb.org

Author Madison Karr

Madison Karr is a student at Baylor University in Waco, Texas. Iam the Lamb is her first published book, but she has enjoyed creative writing since she was very young, especially poetry. She aspires to continue writing children's books.

In addition to writing, Madison enjoys traveling, yoga, boating, surfing, hiking, and just being in the great outdoors. She was inspired to write this children's book by her mom, Stephanie, who is full of brilliant ideas. Her dad, Ted, also played a big role in making this dream become reality.

Illustrator Jamie Ruthenberg

Jamie Ruthenberg is a Detroit-born author, artist, and illustrator. Currently, she is both the author and illustrator of the Miles Educational Series. As a self-taught artist, Jamie creates her illustrations with a number two pencil and watercolor paint. Since her launch into the world of illustration in 2015, her detailed artwork has filled the pages of over 12 books, many of which are discussed on her YouTube series, Jamie's Book and a Bite, as well as on her new book reading series.